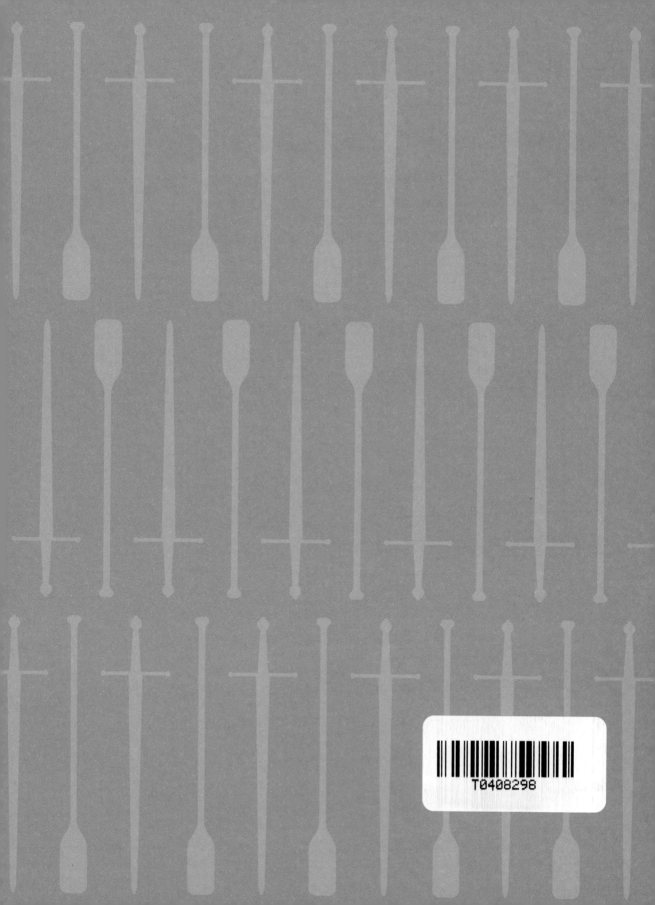

"For years, I lived in Edinburgh, just steps from the historic John Knox House and St. Giles' Cathedral. Yet, there was so much about his life I never knew. Sinclair Ferguson's new children's book on John Knox reveals fascinating details about his early years, offering an engaging glimpse into the man behind the Scottish Reformation. Perfect for young readers, the Do Great Things for God series is an excellent introduction to church history while providing faithful encouragement for both children and adults."

MELISSA KRUGER, Author, *Wherever You Go, I Want You to Know;*
Vice President of Discipleship Programming, The Gospel Coalition

"I will definitely be reading this book to my children, about an influential Scottish minister called Knox by an influential Scottish minister called Ferguson. A great read on one of the heroes of our (Reformed) faith!"

JONNY GIBSON, Associate Professor of Old Testament, Westminster Theological Seminary, Philadelphia; Author, *My First ABC Book of Bible Verses* and *Be Thou My Vision*

"This is not just a great little introduction to a hero of the faith. It is a wonderful encouragement for children, showing that the Lord really is sufficient for every situation, that he is faithful, and that he does, in truth, use all things for the good of those who love him."

MICHAEL REEVES, President and Professor of Theology, Union School of Theology; Author, *Delighting in the Trinity* and *Come, You Weary: Enjoy Christ's Comfort*

John Knox
© Sinclair Ferguson 2025.

Illustrated by Cecilia Messina | Design and Art Direction by André Parker
Series Concept by Laura Caputo-Wickham

"The Good Book For Children" is an imprint of The Good Book Company Ltd
thegoodbook.com | thegoodbook.co.uk | thegoodbook.com.au | thegoodbook.co.nz
ISBN: 9781802543186 | JOB-008303 | Printed in India

Do Great Things for God

John Knox

The Boy Who Changed a Country

Sinclair Ferguson

Illustrated by Cecilia Messina

Welcome to the
Do Great Things for God
Series!

In each of these books, you will meet someone who, in some ways, was very ordinary, just like you and me. Sometimes they were brave, sometimes they were scared, and sometimes they made mistakes.

But in other ways the person you're about to meet was very *extra*ordinary – because they knew that God is great and they wanted to serve God, and God used them to do great things.

So enjoy meeting John Knox!

Young John Knox was bored. He was growing up in Haddington in the south-east of Scotland in the 1530s, and it was his daily Latin lesson. He was good at Latin, but he didn't really like it. And he didn't like people asking, "John, What are you going to do when you grow up?"

"Will I become a priest?" he wondered. "Or a teacher? Or a lawyer? Or will I become a soldier who carries a sword, and fight the English next time the Scottish army faces them in battle?"

John did become a priest—and a lawyer, and a teacher. And for a while he did carry a sword.

But first he went to St Andrews University. Then he became a priest who was a lawyer and a teacher!

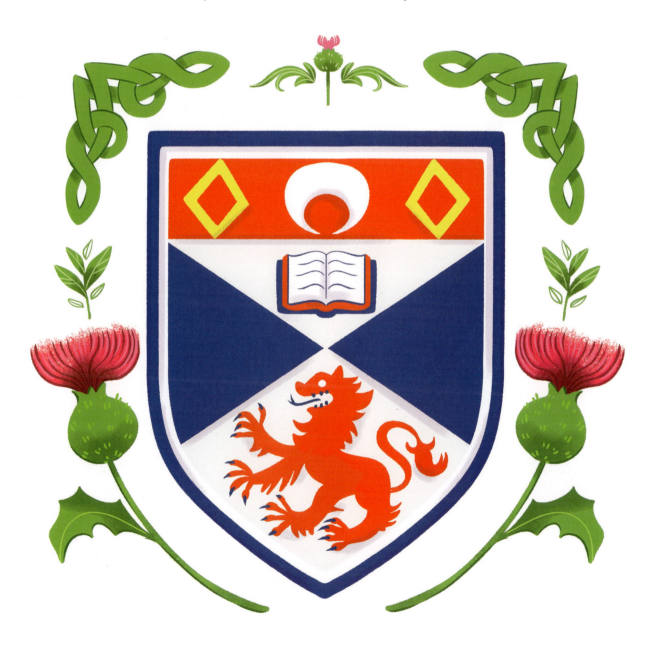

Although he was busy, John did not feel at peace. Although he was doing lots of good things, saying his prayers, and going to church, he wasn't sure he was going to go to heaven when he died.

Then John discovered in the Bible that Jesus had died to forgive his sins and wanted John to be with him in heaven! And Jesus had prayed for him! Now John trusted Jesus as his Saviour and Lord.

One day John heard a man preach about Jesus from God's word – from the Bible. His name was George Wishart. Soon John went everywhere with him.
Some people didn't like George's preaching. So John became his bodyguard. He even carried a big sword!

But then George's enemies captured him. They took him to St Andrews. On 1 March 1546 he was cruelly killed outside the castle walls.

Not long after that, some brave people seized that castle and started a church inside it!

But all over Scotland, everyone who loved God's word was in danger. So at Easter time in 1547, John and some boys who he had begun to teach joined the church in the castle at St Andrews. It seemed the safest place to be.

When the people heard John teaching from the Bible, they asked him to be their preacher!

But soon afterwards, French warships attacked the castle. Scottish soldiers fired cannonballs at it from inside the town! John and his friends surrendered and came out of the castle.

They were chained up and forced to row a French warship. Can you imagine how horrible that must have been?

After nineteen long months John was set free. He went to live in England.

The young English king, Edward VI, loved God's word and made John one of his own special preachers.

KING EDWARD VI
1547 - 1553

But then Edward became ill and died. His half-sister Mary became Queen – and she hated what John preached. Now it was dangerous for John to be in Scotland *and* England. So he escaped to Germany and then went to Switzerland.

With his friends he produced a famous Bible called "The Geneva Bible." It contained brief notes to help explain the Bible's message.

John wrote letters to encourage Christians who were still in Scotland to keep trusting and following the Lord Jesus.

By 1559, John thought it would be safe enough to go home. He sailed back to Scotland and arrived there in May.

John never left Scotland again. He travelled about preaching. Many people came to believe in Jesus. He became minister of a church in Edinburgh, near the castle there. And with five friends (all called "John") he wrote The Scots Confession, a little book that helped people understand the Bible's teaching.

The Queen of Scotland didn't like John's preaching about Jesus — but John didn't let that stop him. He loved Jesus, cared for the poor, and helped churches get ministers and lots of schools get teachers!

Sometimes John returned to St Andrews. The students liked to watch him walking down the street. They knew he loved Jesus and had suffered for the gospel.

On the last day of John's life in 1572, he asked his wife, Margaret, to read the Bible passage that had helped him to trust in Jesus all those years before. So she read John 17, where Jesus prays for his followers:

"Father, I desire that they also, whom you have given me, may be with me where I am, to see my glory that you have given me..." (v 24)

If we trust in Jesus we can say, "Jesus prayed for me. He loves me and he wants me to be in heaven with him." John Knox discovered that. For days he was under attack in a castle. For months he had to row a French warship. For years he was in danger and had to live far from home. Now, he is enjoying being with Jesus for ever.

And we can be with Jesus for ever too, if we trust him as our Saviour and Lord.

John Knox

1514 – 1572

"Father, I desire that they also, whom you have given me, may be with me where I am, to see my glory that you have given me..."
John 17 v 24

Questions to Think About

1. Which part of John's story did you like best?

2. John and his Christian friends were forced to row a French warship. They probably prayed together when they could, and reminded each other that they could still trust God. Can you think of a Bible story or verse that would help you to trust God in that situation?

3. John helped to produce the Geneva Bible, which included answers to people's questions. Who most helps you to find the answers to your questions about the Bible? Thank God for them now.

4. What ideas does John's story give you about how you might serve Jesus when you are older?

5. What is one truth about God that you'd like to remember from this story?

John Knox

1514 John Knox is born in Haddington in south-east Scotland (probably – his date of birth is not completely certain).

1536 John leaves St Andrews University and becomes a priest.

1543 John realises that the Bible says people are saved and forgiven by trusting Jesus and not by what they do. He becomes a "Protestant"—someone who disagreed with what the Catholic church was teaching about how to be saved.

1545 Becomes bodyguard to the preacher George Wishart. Wishart is killed a year later.

1547 John goes to St Andrews Castle and preaches there. When the castle falls, he is forced to row on a French ship for 19 months.

1549 John is released from the French ship and goes to Berwick (in England, on the border with Scotland) and works as a pastor there.

1554 Mary I becomes queen of England. She is a Catholic and starts imprisoning Protestants. John goes into hiding and a year later escapes to Europe. He ends up in Geneva, Switzerland.

1555 John gets married to Marjory Bowes. He secretly returns to Scotland.

1556 John travels round Scotland, preaching from the Bible. He is condemned as a "heretic" (someone who teaches seriously wrong things about God). His life is in danger, so he returns to Geneva.

1559 John returns to Scotland again and becomes the leader of the Scottish Protestants. He preaches a sermon about worshipping God in the way the Bible tells us to. It starts a rebellion against the Catholic rulers of Scotland.

1560 Scotland becomes a Protestant country, but John's wife, Marjory, dies.

1561 John becomes the minister of St Giles' Cathedral in Edinburgh, the capital city of Scotland.

1564 John gets married again, to Margaret Stewart.

1566 John writes one of his most important books, *The History of the Reformation in Scotland*.

1572 John dies in Edinburgh and is buried at St Giles' Cathedral.

Interact With John's Story!

Download Free Resources at
thegoodbook.com/kids-resources

Do Great Things for God

Inspiring Biographies for Young Children

 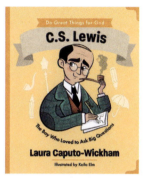 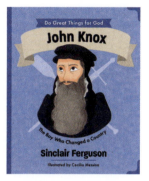 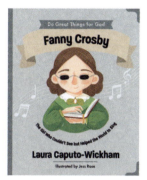

  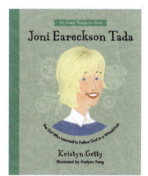 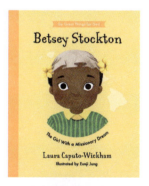

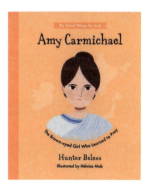   

thegoodbook.com | thegoodbook.co.uk

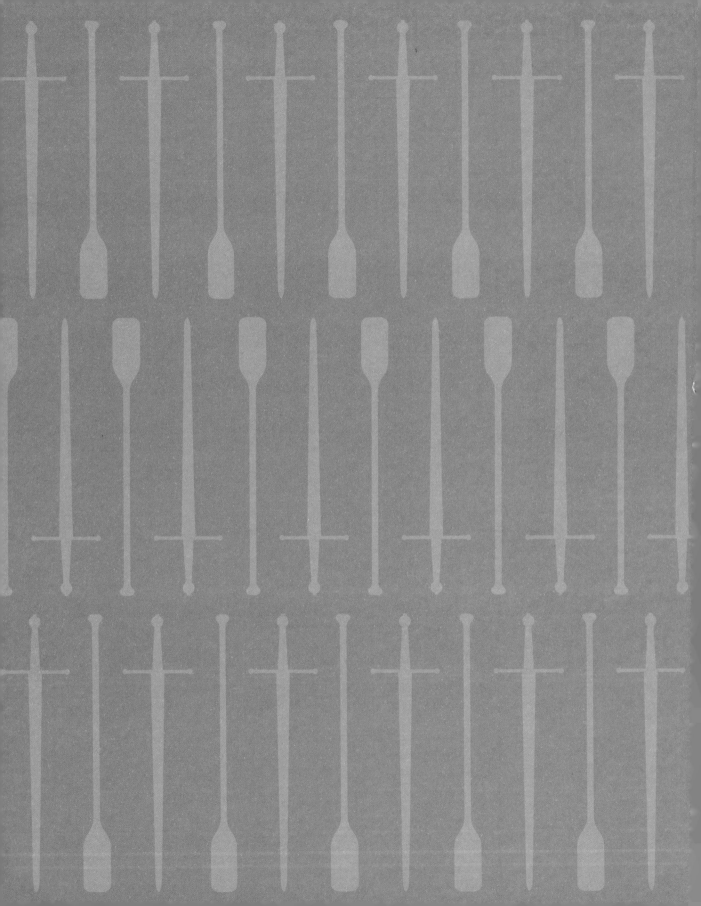